leading
with love

leading with love

Inspiration for Spiritual Activists

ILLUSTRATIONS BY MAUDE WHITE

EDITED BY HISAE MATSUDA

**PARALLAX
PRESS**

BERKELEY, CALIFORNIA

Parallax Press
P.O. Box 7355
Berkeley, California 94707
parallax.org

Parallax Press is the publishing division of
Plum Village Community of Engaged Buddhism
Text © 2018 Parallax Press
Artwork © 2018 Maude White
All rights reserved
Printed in Canada

Cover and text design by Jess Morphew
Illustrations © 2018 Maude White
Photographs of artwork © 2018 Gary Gold
Illustrator photo © Mallory D'Alessandro
Editor photo © Hisae Matsuda
Translation of song text of "De noche" ("At Night")
© Ateliers et Presses de Taizé, Taizé, France
Excerpt from "You Worry Too Much" by Jalal ad-Din Rumi, reprinted
with permission of Jain Publishing Company, Fremont, California
"The Peace of Wild Things" © 2012 by Wendell Berry, reprinted with
permission of Counterpoint Press, Berkeley, California

ISBN: 978-1-946764-37-9

Library of Congress Cataloging-in-Publication Data
is available upon request.

1 2 3 4 5 / 22 21 20 19 18

To my mother, who is a compass and a beacon —MW

To Meia, Leo, and Nina —HM

Contents

Preface

*If you are a poet, you will see clearly that there
is a cloud floating in this sheet of paper.*

—THICH NHAT HANH

These words are printed on the calendar above
my desk at Parallax Press, and they are also next
to my writing table at home. They remind me that
no matter how divided or separate we may feel in
our activism, spirituality, work, or family lives, in
reality we are always interconnected. As someone
who earns her livelihood editing books, paper—
that dry, flat medium pressed from the flesh of trees

and other plants—has a special meaning for me. But its significance goes deeper. Paper was a precious substance in ancient cultures, the main means humankind has had for centuries to keep and continue its stories from one generation to another. It is sacred. If you were to visit my native Japan, for example, you would see shrines and sacred trees garlanded with cut-and-folded paper zig-zags called *shide*, representing bolts of lightning; in ceremonies, priests purify you by waving not a smudge stick, but a wand tasseled with these same paper shide. In his book *Awakening of the Heart*, Zen teacher and Parallax founder Thich Nhat Hanh writes how a sheet of paper does more than symbolize the sacred; it contains the whole universe within it:

> Without a cloud, there will be no rain; without rain, the trees cannot grow; and without trees, we cannot make paper.

The cloud is essential for the paper to exist. . . . If we look into this sheet of paper even more deeply, we can see the sunshine in it. If the sunshine is not there, the forest cannot grow. In fact, nothing can grow. Even we cannot grow without sunshine . . . .

You cannot point out one thing that is not here—time, space, the earth, the rain, the minerals in the soil, the sunshine, the cloud, the river, the heat. Everything coexists with this sheet of paper. . . . This sheet of paper is, because everything else is. [*]

How wonderful, then, that in this book of quotes by and for spiritual activists we are able to include these cut-paper art pieces by

---

[*] Thich Nhat Hanh, *Awakening of the Heart: Essential Buddhist Sutras and Commentaries* (Berkeley, CA: Parallax Press, 2011), 413.

New York artist Maude White. Using nothing more than a blank sheet of paper and a very sharp X-Acto knife, Maude reveals images that convey the intricacy and interconnectedness of existence. "I believe very strongly that art can heal," Maude writes in her artist's statement, "art can be a gentle conduit, a precious, living thing that can enter both creator and viewer and thereby extend them and connect them. . . ."

Maude, like some of the people quoted in this book, is an "artivist" whose intention is to inspire and not merely to illustrate. "My work is created with love for the primary purpose of sharing love and encouraging love between others," she says. "I am not creating for art's sake."

The editors at Parallax Press and I have chosen the quotes in this book with a similar intention of sharing voices of healing, love, and connection, especially during these dark days. The number of refugees from wars, environmental destruction, poverty, and societal breakdown in our world is unprecedented in history. As a species, we humans are finally becoming aware that we need to find new ways to take care of each other, ourselves, and our planet to survive and thrive.

Here are words from some of the most prominent inspirations of the modern peace movement—Mahatma Gandhi, Dr. Martin Luther King Jr., His Holiness the Dalai Lama, and Thich Nhat Hanh and his students—people who have forged their spirituality in the fire of open conflict, war, and injustice. Sometimes the battlefield is an inner one in the form of personal, familial, or generational trauma; we also chose quotes from people who work courageously in their communities with little recognition or who use a deeply personal practice to transfigure their pain into beauty through their art. Some of the people we chose to quote are household names, while others are relatively unknown. They all share the trait of standing up for truth and love, sometimes at great personal risk. Following in the Parallax Press tradition of publishing people who bring beauty and joy into their work for peace and justice, we've also included visionaries of social change who are poets, gardeners, artists, singers, musicians, cooks, teachers, farmers, and writers.

These quotes are for activists who know they'll burn out without self-care, mindfulness, and compassion, who need to hear words of encouragement and to know that they are not alone. Words are powerful, and the right words at the right time can uplift and inspire us during the most difficult experiences life may bring.

May these words on paper remind you of our interconnectedness. There is a community of people who are walking alongside us, from all over the world and throughout history, inspiring and supporting us as we move forward into a future we can't yet imagine, but which we know exists, about to be realized in the present moment.

Hisae Matsuda
January 2018
Richmond, California

Awakening

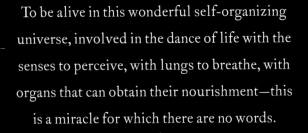

To be alive in this wonderful self-organizing universe, involved in the dance of life with the senses to perceive, with lungs to breathe, with organs that can obtain their nourishment—this is a miracle for which there are no words.

JOANNA MACY

Go into nature, fall back in love with
the natural world, and let your commitment
stem from that place of connection.
What you see may spark a powerful connection
that will motivate you into action.

XIUHTEZCATL
MARTINEZ

Do you have a body?
Don't sit on the porch!
Go out and walk in the rain!
If you are in love,
then why are you asleep?
Wake up, wake up!
You have slept millions and millions of years.
Why not wake up this morning?

FRAGMENTS OF
POEMS BY KABIR,
chosen by brother David Steindl-Rast

Every moment is
an organizing opportunity,
every person a potential activist,
every minute a chance
to change the world.

DOLORES HUERTA

Love seeketh not itself to please,
Nor for itself hath any care,
But for another gives its ease,
And builds a heaven in hell's despair.

WILLIAM BLAKE

Words are power.
And a book
is full of words.
Be careful what power
you get from it.
But know that you do.

YOKO ONO

Flaubert called himself a human pen; I would say that I am a human ear. When I walk down the street and catch words, phrases, and exclamations ... I love how humans talk ... I love the lone human voice. It is my greatest love and passion. The road [here] has been long—almost forty years, going from person to person, from voice to voice. I can't say that I have always been up to following this path. Many times I have been shocked and frightened by human beings. I have experienced delight and revulsion. I have sometimes wanted to forget what I heard, to return to a time when I lived in ignorance. More than once, however, I have seen the sublime in people, and wanted to cry.

SVETLANA ALEXIEVICH

To be aware of the wonder and
enchantment of the world, its astonishing
creatures and complex interactions,
and to be aware simultaneously of the
remarkably rapid destruction of almost every
living system, is to take on a burden of
grief that is almost unbearable.

GEORGE MONBIOT

In Buddhism, there is a lot of emphasis on meditating on the truth of suffering. This may be a bit depressing, but when we see our faults clearly, we also see the possibility of freeing ourselves from them. Seeing our faults has very much to do with our capacity for awakening.

HIS HOLINESS
THE DALAI LAMA

We, unaccustomed to courage
exiles from delight
live coiled in shells of loneliness
until love leaves its high holy temple
and comes into our sight
to liberate us into life.

MAYA ANGELOU

The hum of drones has returned, I can hear them hovering over our heads, choosing their next prey. It's very hot. Jaffa is crying. My mother-in-law warns the kids not to touch her blessed plants. I write an essay that starts with the words "We are OK in Gaza." But it's a lie, we are never OK. Nonetheless, hope is what you have even at the worst of times. It is the only thing that can't be stripped from you. The only part of you the drones or the F16s or the tanks or the warships can't reach. So you hug it to yourself. You do not let it go. The moment you give it up, you lose the most precious thing that nature and your humanity have endowed you with. Hope is your only weapon.

ATEF ABU SAIF

No one is born hating another person because of the color of his skin or his background or his religion. People learn to hate, and if they can learn to hate, they can be taught to love, for love comes more naturally to the human heart than its opposite.

NELSON MANDELA

We are here to awaken
from the illusion
of our separateness.

THICH NHAT HANH

If there is one who's not free, then I am not free.
If there is one who suffers, then I suffer.

AI WEIWEI

By night we hasten, in darkness
to search for living water
only our thirst leads us onward
only our thirst leads us onward

TAIZÉ CHANT

I reflect on my childhood experience when I would visit a stream next to our home to fetch water for my mother. I would drink water straight from the stream. Playing among the arrowroot leaves I tried in vain to pick up the strands of frogs' eggs, believing they were beads. But every time I put my little fingers under them they would break. Later, I saw thousands of tadpoles: black, energetic, and wriggling through the clear water against the background of the brown earth. This is the world I inherited from my parents.

Today, over fifty years later, the stream has dried up, women walk long distances for water, which is not always clean, and children will never know what they have lost. The challenge is to restore the home of the tadpoles and give back to our children a world of beauty and wonder.

WANGARI MAATHAI

The premise for empathy has to be equal
humanity; it is an injustice to demand
that the maligned identify with those who
question their humanity.

CHIMANANDA
NGOZI ADICHIE

If you need me to prove my humanity,
I'm not the one who's not human.

SUHAIYMAH
MANZOOR-KHAN

Don't beg for your dignity
and your humanity.

TARANA BURKE

When they started talking about
eight to ten years in prison, I couldn't
stay calm anymore. I repeated these
three things every day:
"Perseverance,
bravery,
endurance."
I said this in the morning, each time I
was taken out for interrogation, and
before sleeping at night. I relied on
this mantra to get by.

LI MAIZI

Only the willfully blind can ignore that the history of human existence is simultaneously the history of pain: of brutality, murder, mass extinction, every form of venality and cyclical horror. No land is free of it; no people are without their bloodstain; no tribe entirely innocent. But there is still this redeeming matter of incremental progress. It might look small to those with apocalyptic perspectives, but to she who not so long ago could not vote, or drink from the same water fountain as her fellow citizens, or marry the person she chose, or live in a certain neighborhood, such incremental change feels enormous.

ZADIE SMITH

What if we loved all the babies fiercely
Loving the ones above and below certain global
    southern borders equally
Giving them access to the same opportunities
Because we've done away with the models of
    scarcity
Because we know the truth of love's infinite
    possibilities
What if we all worked until this vision
succeeded
I believe this world is possible
I see it with the eye of my heart
I write from that place when I create my art
The place where we'd no longer need diplomacy
Or politicians who are conscious socially
    because we'd all be
I've been to the future
It lives in the arms of my mother
I've returned to share this better way

MONA HAYDAR

When I climbed up in that tree I was new to activism, but I soon realized that we had become so good at defining what we were against that what we were against was beginning to define us. I saw the problem in meetings where activists were "clear-cutting" each other with their words and their anger. As people were talking I could literally hear the chainsaws in their words, cutting each other apart. I saw that peace rallies had become anti-war rallies, places where I couldn't even walk up close to the rally because of the way people were speaking through the megaphone: it sounded like they were dropping bombs.

This all became clear to me about halfway through my time in the tree, when I was

experiencing a lot of pain and really felt like I was falling apart. That's when I went deeper and realized I had climbed up in the tree not because I was angry at corporations and governments—although I was angry at them—but because I loved the forest and I loved the planet and I loved this sacred life that we're all a part of. And so I began to approach all the issues from that place of love.

JULIA BUTTERFLY HILL

Imagining

Poetry is the way
we help give name
to the nameless so it can
be thought.

AUDRE LORDE

How can you make your life sustainable—
physically, emotionally, financially,
intellectually, spiritually?

Are you helping create communities rooted
in values of sustainability, including
environmental and cultural sustainability?

Do you feel that you have enough time
and space to take in thoughts and images and
experiences of things that are joyful
and nourishing?

What are your resources when you
feel isolated or powerless?

MUSHIM PATRICIA IKEDA

Connection is why we're here.
It's what gives purpose and
meaning to our lives. . . .
It doesn't matter whether you
talk to people who work in social
justice and mental health and abuse
and neglect— what we know is
that connection, the ability to feel
connected, is neurobiologically how
we're wired. It's why we're here.

BRENÉ BROWN

Since the appearance of visible life on Earth,
380 million years had to elapse
in order for a butterfly to learn how to fly;
180 million years to create a rose
with no other commitment than to be beautiful;
and four geological eras in order for us human beings
to be able to sing better than birds,
and to be able to die from love.
It is not honorable for the human talent,
in the golden age of science,
to have conceived the way
for such an ancient and colossal process
to return to the nothingness from which it came
through the simple act of pushing a button.

GABRIEL GARCÍA MÁRQUEZ

To prevent the next war, we have to practice peace today. If we establish peace in our hearts, in our way of looking at things, and in our way of being with each other and with the world, then we are doing our best to make sure the next war will not come. War is the fruit of our collective consciousness. If we wait until another war is imminent to begin to practice peace, it will be too late. Peace begins here, now.

THICH NHAT HANH

Nibi [water] is who we are and what we are made of. Our first teaching on water begins in our mother's womb. We all have this teaching; we can't live in our mother's womb without water. All of us would not be sitting here without water. It makes me sad when I think about the water; I'm sad because our waters are sick, not just here in Canada, but all over the world. . . . Mother Earth was in existence for billions of years and she doesn't need us. We need her. It's time for humanity to stop terrorizing Mother Earth and give her time to heal.

AUTUMN PELTIER

Information is
not power.
Power is power.
Action is what turns
information into power.

RINKU SEN

Like a beautiful brightly colored flower
     without fragrance
Is the well-spoken word without action.
Like the beautiful brightly colored flower full
     of fragrance
Is the well-spoken word and the deed that
     matches the word.

DHAMMAPADA 4, 8–9

Whenever I do anything, I see the eyes of my parents and grandparents in me. When I worked with villagers, I always had the impression that I was doing the work together with them and also with the loving hands of those friends who saved a handful of rice or a few dong to support the work. My hands were their hands. My love was the wonderful love of the network of ancestors, parents, relatives, and friends born in me. The work I have done is the work of everyone. It is not just my work.

SISTER CHAN KHONG

I believe that
children's souls
are the inheritors of
historical memory
from previous
generations.

HAYAO MIYAZAKI

One can never leave
what one leaves behind.

CARLA TRUJILLO

By trying to feed the Holy in Nature the fruit of beauty from the tree of memory of our indigenous souls, grown in the composted failures of our past need to conquer, watered by the tears of cultural grief, we might become ancestors worth descending from and possibly grow a place of hope for a time beyond our own.

MARTÍN PRECHTEL

We are a part
of everything that is
beneath us, above us,
and around us.
Our past is our present,
our present is our future,
and our future is
seven generations past
and present.

WINONA LADUKE

As Jimmy Boggs used to remind us, revolutions are made out of love for people and for place. He often talked about loving America enough to change it. "I love this country," he used to say, "not only because my ancestors' blood is in the soil but because of what I believe it can become." Love isn't just something you feel. It's something you do every day when you go out and pick up the paper and bottles scattered the night before on the corner, when you stop and talk to a neighbor, when you argue passionately for what you believe in with whoever will listen, when you call a friend to see how they're doing, when you write a letter to the newspaper, when you give a speech and give 'em hell, when you never stop believing that we can all be more than what we are. In other words, love isn't about what we did yesterday; it's about what we do today and tomorrow and the day after.

GRACE LEE BOGGS

Most people view themselves as waves and forget they are also water. They are used to living in the realm of birth and death, and they forget about the realm of no birth and no death. Just as a wave lives the life of water, so too do we live the life of no birth and no death. We need to know this, and to be in touch with the reality ... the word *know* here is very important. To know is to realize. Realization is mindfulness. All the work of meditation is aimed at awakening us in order to know one thing: that birth and death can never touch us in any way whatsoever.

THICH NHAT HANH

A friend sent me a photo
of a beautiful star twinkling
in the night sky.
"I found an old picture
of you," she wrote.
"Here you are a trillion years ago."
When a star explodes at the end
of its life, it scatters its elements
throughout the universe,
and that is what forms planets.
We're literally made of stardust.
It really was a picture of me,
and of everyone.

SPRING WASHAM

Like slavery and apartheid, poverty is not natural. It is man-made and it can be overcome and eradicated by the actions of human beings. And overcoming poverty is not a gesture of charity. It is an act of justice. It is the protection of a fundamental human right, the right to dignity and a decent life. While poverty persists, there is no true freedom.

NELSON MANDELA

You may wonder if
the most wonderful
moments of your life
are already behind you.
Or you may think the
happiest moment of
your life is still to come.
But this is the moment
we have been waiting for.

THICH NHAT HANH

Truth-Telling & Transformation

What I know for sure is that speaking your truth is the most powerful tool we all have. And I am especially proud and inspired by all the women who have felt strong enough and empowered enough to speak up and share their personal stories.

OPRAH WINFREY

Love and truth are faces of the same coin, and both very difficult to practice, and the only things worth living for....

True love is boundless like the ocean and, swelling within one, spreads itself out and, crossing all boundaries and frontiers, envelops the entire world.

MAHATMA GANDHI

Radical transformation
of society requires
personal and spiritual
change first or at least
simultaneously.

SULAK SIVARAKSA

In the face of the tremendous suffering of the world, there is a joy that comes from not denying the pain, but from sitting in meditation, even when it is difficult, and letting our hearts open to the experience. It is the nitty-gritty work of practice to sit here and feel your sadness and my sadness and our fear, desperation, and restlessness, to open to them and begin to learn that to love is to die to how we wanted it to be, and to open more to its truth. To love is to accept. It is not a weakness. It is the most extraordinary power.

True love is really the same as awareness. True love is to see the divine goodness, the Buddha nature, the truth of each moment, and to say, "Yes," to allow ourselves to open, to accept. That is our practice every moment, whether in sitting meditation or action meditation. To be aware, to see the truth, frees us. It opens us to what is now, to what is here, and we see it as it is.

JACK KORNFIELD

We realize the importance of our voices only when we are silenced.

MALALA YOUSAFZAI

Lying is done
with words, and also
with silence.

ADRIENNE RICH

Now is the time to counter lies with facts, repeatedly and unflaggingly, while also proclaiming the greater truths: of our equal humanity, of decency, of compassion. Every precious ideal must be reiterated, every obvious argument made, because an ugly idea left unchallenged begins to turn the color of normal. It does not have to be like this.

CHIMANANDA
NGOZI ADICHIE

The path to healing
includes transforming
all of our demons.

SPRING WASHAM

If you don't like to
be uncomfortable,
you need to get to the
root of what you're
uncomfortable with.

ALICIA GARZA

Throughout human history, the impulse to destroy what we are afraid of has taken a heavy toll on wild creatures of all kinds, from bears and wolves to rattlesnakes and bees. Meeting our fears with loving-kindness—allowing compassion and curiosity to prevail over fear and phobia—may be one of the central tasks of our humanity.

TAI MOSES

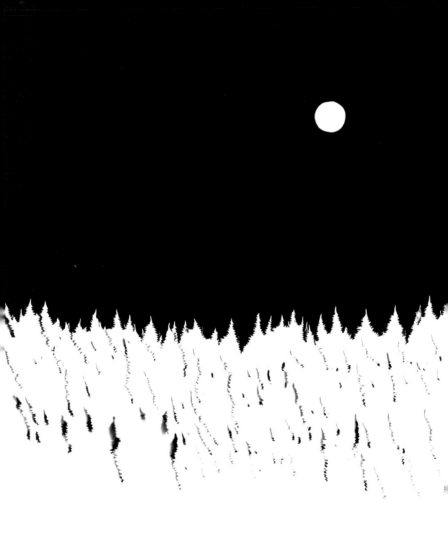

Earth is humankind's
unblinking witness.

HEATHER LYN MANN

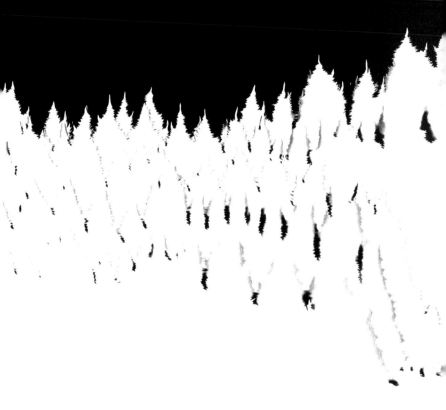

I couldn't control how much money people were contributing [to other candidates], but I could control what I was doing. I could control how hard I was working. And I made sure that no one would knock on more doors than our campaign, both in the primary and in the general election. This year, we knocked on 75,000 doors. And obviously, that means that you knock on the same doors repeatedly. You have to, because not every person answers the door the first time around, and people need to be reminded to go vote. So you have the persuasion knock, then you have the reminder knock, all that sort of stuff. The way I see it is, the thing that was in my control was how aggressively I would knock on doors, and the other thing that is so important is how many quality conversations you have at the door. It is not enough to just leave literature, a flyer, at someone's door and hope that they vote for you. That's not how it works. You have to actually have conversations with people.

DANICA ROEM

Movements are born of
critical connections rather
than critical mass.

GRACE LEE BOGGS

Tips on surviving
the regime:
Respect yourself and
speak for others.
Do one small thing
every day to prove the
existence of justice.

AI WEIWEI

Love is really sacrifice. It's actually not vocal. Although it can be enunciated, it has to be practiced. You need both. . . . It's very easy to be a servant, but very difficult to be of service. When you are of service, you're there whether you like it or not, whether it's Sunday, Monday, or a holiday. You're there whenever you're needed.

CÉSAR CHÁVEZ

We must discover
the power of love, the
power, the redemptive
power of love.
And when we discover
that, we will be able to
make of this old world
a new world. . . .
Love is the only way.

MARTIN LUTHER
KING, JR.

The basic sources of happiness are a
good heart, compassion, and love.
If we have these, even if we are surrounded by
hostility, we will feel little disturbance.

HIS HOLINESS
THE DALAI LAMA

Hatred has never stopped hatred.
Only love stops hate.
This is the eternal law.

DHAMMAPADA I, 3 – 5

Hatred ever kills; love never dies. Such is the
vast difference between the two. What is obtained by love is obtained for all time. What is
obtained by hatred proves a burden in reality, for
it increases hatred. The duty of a human being
is to diminish hatred and to promote love.

MAHATMA GANDHI

Darkness cannot
drive out darkness;
only light can do that.
Hate cannot drive
out hate; only love
can do that.

MARTIN LUTHER
KING, JR.

We extend ourselves only so far as it doesn't intrude upon our own comfort zone. As long as we continue to practice in that way, we'll still be disturbed by all sorts of political, economic, and social challenges as well as by our own personal crises.

If we want to truly be happy, truly be free, we have to extend ourselves beyond our comfort zone, to all beings, in all situations . . . we have to move beyond considering Dharma practice to be, as one person put it, "a self-improvement project" and recognize that the essence . . . is the improvement of the welfare of all. . . .

We develop greater confidence in facing situations that might appear scary, uncomfortable, or inconvenient; we develop the guts to deal with whatever challenges life hands us.

TSOKNYI RINPOCHE

All that you touch, you change.
All that you change, changes you.
The only lasting truth is change.

OCTAVIA BUTLER

Tenderness

Love takes off the masks
that we fear we cannot live without
and know we cannot
live within.

JAMES BALDWIN

I don't feel powerful at all. . . .
Maybe being powerful
means to be fragile.

AI WEIWEI

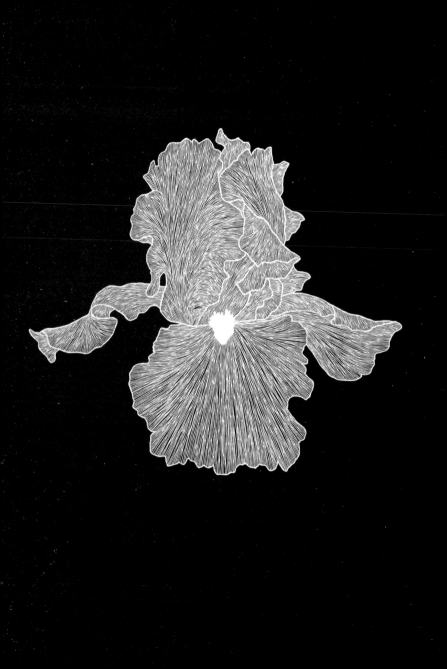

Although it was already late at night, I sat on my bed box in the dark and massaged my hands. One hand tended the other, and then in turn was tended for. . . . Thank you, hands, for being here to help me embrace someone, to write words of trust and empathy, to lift a pot of rice, to make a gesture.

SISTER DANG NGHIEM

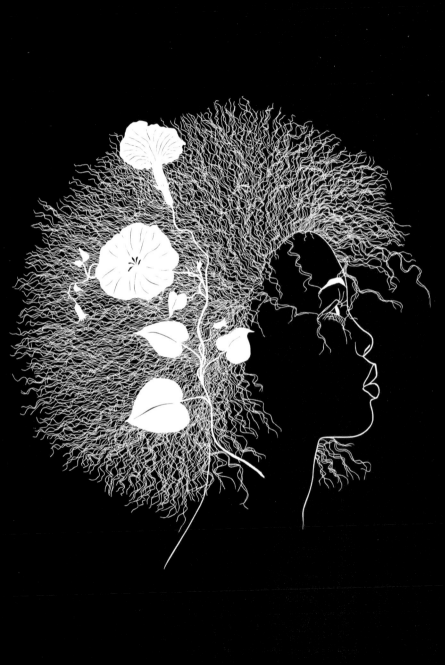

I think our notions of what counts as radical have changed over time. Self-care and healing and attention to the body and the spiritual dimension—all of this is now a part of radical social justice struggles. That wasn't the case before. And I think that now we're thinking deeply about the connection between interior life and what happens in the social world. . . .

We have to imagine the kind of society we want to inhabit. We can't simply assume that somehow, magically, we're going to create a new society in which there will be new human beings. No, we have to begin that process of creating the society we want to inhabit right now.

ANGELA DAVIS

Sharing views includes sharing our experience. . . . It is important not just to share positive things that are happening to us, but our mistakes as well, asking others for help when needed.

SISTER ANNABEL LAITY

Be sincere in your prayers.
Sincerity is humility, and
you will acquire humility only
by accepting humiliations.
All that has been said
about humility is not enough
to teach you humility.
All that you have read about
humility is not enough to
teach you humility.
You learn humility only by
accepting humiliations.

MOTHER TERESA

My years of struggling against inequality, abusive power, poverty, oppression, and injustice had finally revealed something to me about myself. Being close to suffering, death, executions, and cruel punishments didn't just illuminate the brokenness of others; in a moment of anguish and heartbreak, it also exposed my own brokenness. You can't effectively fight abusive power, poverty, inequality, illness, oppression, or injustice and not be broken by it.

We are all broken by something. We have all hurt someone and have been hurt. We all share the condition of brokenness even if our brokenness is not equivalent. . . .

I guess I'd always known but never fully considered that being broken is what makes us human. We all have our reasons. Sometimes we're fractured by the choices we make; sometimes we're shattered by things we would never have chosen. But our brokenness is also the source of our common humanity, the basis for our shared search for comfort, meaning, and healing. Our shared vulnerability and imperfection nurtures and sustains our capacity for compassion.

BRYAN STEVENSON

The more you destroy
another human being,
the more you destroy yourself.

MUBARAK AWAD

My right to be me is tied
with a thousand threads to
your right to be you.

LESLIE FEINBERG

I know that I stopped thinking about extreme grief as the sole vehicle for great art when the grief started to take people with it. . . . The tortured artist is the artist that gets remembered for all time, particularly if they either perish or overcome. But the truth is that so many of us are stuck in the middle. So many of us begin tortured and end tortured, with only brief bursts of light in between, and I'd rather have average art and survival than miracles that come at the cost of someone's life.

HANIF WILLIS-
ABDURRAQIB

In my world, there always seems to be way too much to do, along with too much suffering and societal corruption and not enough spaces of deep rest and regeneration.

When I get desperate, which is pretty often, I ask myself how to not be overwhelmed by despair or cynicism. For my own sake, for my family, and for my sangha, I need to vow to not burn out. And I ask others to vow similarly so they'll be around when I need them for support. In fact, I've formulated a "Great Vow for Mindful Activists":

Aware of suffering and injustice, I, _____,
am working to create a more just, peaceful, and
sustainable world. I promise, for the benefit of
all, to practice self-care, mindfulness, healing,
and joy. I vow to not burn out.

MUSHIM PATRICIA IKEDA

The cure for burnout? Learn to say no, learn to say yes, do something meaningful, walk away from toxic people and organizations, rest, sleep, play, and allow yourself to be vulnerable. Grieve when you need to. Find your rhythm.

ALESSANDRA PIGNI

Metta is the medicine that transforms anger, sorrow, and numbness. To begin, sit down in a quiet place, put your hand on your heart, and focus on self-care, compassion, kindness. Visualize yourself sitting in front of you. Imagine that you are inhaling peace and exhaling kindness. Feel the love that surrounds you. Then recite, silently or aloud, phrases like, "May I be happy and peaceful. May I be safe and protected wherever I go. May I be healthy and strong in my body. May I live with ease and well-being."

SPRING WASHAM

There is no glimpse
of the light without
walking the path.
You can't get it from
anyone else, nor can you give
it to anyone. Just take whatever
steps seem easiest for you,
and as you take a few steps
it will be easier for you
to take a few more.

PEACE PILGRIM

You change the world
by being yourself.

YOKO ONO

Life is filled with suffering,
but it is also filled with
many wonders, like the
blue sky, the sunshine,
the eyes of a baby.
To suffer is not enough.
We must also be in touch
with the wonders of life.
They are within us and
all around us,
everywhere, any time.

THICH NHAT HANH

When despair for the world grows in me
and I wake in the night at the least sound
in fear of what my life and my children's lives may be,
I go and lie down where the wood drake
rests in his beauty on the water, and the great heron feeds.
I come into the peace of wild things
who do not tax their lives with forethought
of grief. I come into the presence of still water.
And I feel above me the day-blind stars
waiting with their light. For a time
I rest in the grace of the world, and am free.

WENDELL BERRY
"The Peace of Wild Things"

This is my simple religion.
There is no need for complicated
philosophies, not even for temples.
Our own brain,
our own heart is our temple.
The philosophy is kindness.

HIS HOLINESS
THE DALAI LAMA

Leading
with Love

I have decided to stick to love.
Hate is too great a burden to bear.

MARTIN LUTHER
KING, JR.

A smile is the most basic
kind of peace work.

THICH NHAT HANH

For me,
every hour is grace.
And I feel gratitude
in my heart each time
I can meet someone and
look at his or her smile.

ELIE WIESEL

Love won't be tampered with, love won't go away. Push it to one side and it creeps to the other. Throw it in the garbage and it springs up clean. Try to root it out and it only flourishes. Love is a weed, a dandelion that you poison from your heart. The taproots wait. The seeds blow off, ticklish, into a part of the yard you didn't spray. And one day, though you worked, though you prodded out each spiky leaf, you lift your eyes and dozens of fat golden faces bob in the grass.

LOUISE ERDRICH

Inasmuch as love
grows in you,
in so much beauty grows;
for love is itself
the beauty of the soul.

AUGUSTINE OF HIPPO

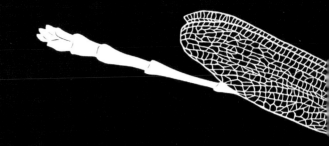

You have seen your own strength.

You have seen your own beauty.

You have seen your golden wings.

Of anything less,

why do you worry?

You are in truth

the soul, of the soul, of the soul.

JALAL AD-DIN RUMI

Where do we find that space of
connecting, of belonging? If you
have love, you have the community
of belonging that comes with it.

BELL HOOKS

Never walk alone. The movement is bigger than one person, so always bring others on board. Everyone has something to offer the struggle.

KASHA JACQUELINE NABAG-
ESERA

When you're working
in concert with others,
your ultimate goal is
everyone moving
toward their highest
expression of self.

Belief systems get
articulated through
the practice of growing
community.

DORIA ROBINSON

Real change will only happen when we fall in love with our planet. Only love can show us how to live in harmony with nature and each other and save us from suffering the devastating effects of climate change.... This is the meaning of love, to be at one. When you love someone, you want to take care of them as you would take care of yourself. When we love the Earth like this, it's a reciprocated love. We'll do anything for the benefit of the Earth, and the Earth will do anything for our well-being.

THICH NHAT HANH

If we are bold, love strikes away the chains of fear from our souls.

MAYA ANGELOU

All at once, my vision shifted and everything was different. Nothing changed in the physical world; the muted light, green vegetation, and black asphalt were as they were a moment ago. Raindrops continued to patter the umbrella. . . .

The most classic teaching describing interbeing (the reality that nothing is truly separate from the whole of everything else) is the metaphor of the ocean and the wave. A wave, trundling merrily along, may think it has a separate self-identity . . . but it is made of water. All waves are made of water, the same water. On that day . . . I caught a glimpse of the reality of our connection. I saw the oneness of the cosmos as a single organism buzzing with joy.

I get it, I thought. I'm looking at the visual reality of the Buddha's teaching on interbeing. And the quivering vibration animating the whole, connecting us all, it's . . . it's love. . . . I'm seeing love, it's a substance and it's everywhere. It's absolute and inviolate. Nothing exists outside of love, so it cannot be harmed.

HEATHER LYN MANN

155

There is an indefinable mysterious power that pervades everything. I feel it though I don't see it. It is this unseen power which makes itself felt and yet defies all proof, because it is unlike all that I perceive through my senses.

I do dimly perceive that whilst everything around me is ever changing and ever dying, there is underlying all that change a living power that is changeless, that holds all together, that creates, dissolves, and recreates. This informing power or spirit is God. To me God is truth and love. God is ethics and morality; God is fearlessness. God is the source of light and life, and yet he is above and beyond all these. God is conscience. He is even the atheism of the atheist.

MAHATMA GANDHI

The common language being spoken is often one of fear. . . . My medicine is the language of love, which creates a space where all people can sit down together. Our world is literally dying for us to become emissaries of love.

JULIA BUTTERFLY HILL

We do not discover the secret of
our lives merely by study
and calculation in our
own isolated meditations.
The meaning of our life is
a secret that has to be revealed
to us in love, by the one we love.
And if this love is unreal, the secret
will not be found, the meaning
will never reveal itself, the message
will never be decoded.
At best, we will receive a scrambled
and partial message, one that will
deceive and confuse us. We will
never be fully real until we let
ourselves fall in love.

THOMAS MERTON

The dandelion is there by the sidewalk,

smiling its wondrous smile,

singing the song of eternity.

Listen. You have ears that can hear it.

Bow your head.

Listen to it.

Leave behind the world of sorrow,

of preoccupation,

and get free.

THICH NHAT HANH

Once you've tasted
freedom, it stays in
your heart and
no one can take it.
Then, you can be
more powerful than a
whole country.

AI WEIWEI

No coming, no going,
no after, no before.
I hold you close to me,
I release you to be so free.
Because I am in you,
and you are in me.
Because I am in you,
and you are in me.

PLUM VILLAGE SONG

Contributors

AI WEIWEI, born in Beijing in 1957, is a Chinese conceptual artist whose art practice isn't separate from his activism. With epic-scale art installations, he calls attention to human rights violations and expands the definition of art to include new forms of social engagement. When he was a year old, his family was sent to a forced labor camp after the political denunciation of his father, poet Ai Qing. The police in his country have imprisoned him, kept him under house arrest and surveillance, bulldozed his new studio, and physically assaulted him, seeing him as a threat to "harmonious society," yet he continues to struggle for freedom of expression and remind us of the power, and even the responsibility, of art to move us to action and change society.

MAYA ANGELOU (1928–2014) was an American poet, memoirist, and civil rights activist. She began writing at the age of forty after a varied career as an actor, dancer, and journalist. Her first book was *I Know Why the Caged Bird Sings*, the first of seven autobiographies; she published dozens of books and was credited with a list of plays, movies, and television shows spanning more than fifty years. Maya Angelou's words promote self-examination, equality, and friendship, and her works continue to inspire a love of truth and to a be reminder of the value of recording personal experience.

AUGUSTINE OF HIPPO (354–430 CE), known as Saint Augustine, was an early North African Christian theologian and philosopher whose writings influenced the development of Western Christianity and philosophy. An indigenous Berber, whose family had long practiced as Roman Christians, after a rebellious youth he returned to his Christian faith and became the bishop of Hippo Regius in what is now Algeria. He is viewed as one of the most important Church Fathers for his writings; among his most important works are *The City of God* and *The Confessions*.

CHIMAMANDA NGOZI ADICHIE was born in Nigeria in 1977. She is the author of three novels and a short story collection. Her 2012 talk "We Should All Be Feminists" sparked a worldwide conversation about changing perceptions of feminism, and was published as a book in 2014. She has received many awards and distinctions, including the Orange Broadband Prize for Fiction in 2007 and a MacArthur Foundation Fellowship in 2008.

SVETLANA ALEXIEVICH, was born in Ivano Frankivsk, Ukraine, in 1948. Her father was Belarusian and her mother, Ukrainian. Alexievich studied journalism at the University of Minsk, and worked as a teacher, investigative journalist, and editor. Her criticism of the political regimes in the Soviet Union and thereafter Belarus has periodically forced her to live abroad. In her books, Svetlana Alexievich depicts life during and after the Soviet Union through the experience of individuals, using interviews to create a collage of a wide range of voices, blurring the boundary between reporting and fiction. She won the 2015 Nobel Prize in Literature.

MUBARAK AWAD was born in Jerusalem in 1943. He is a Palestinian American psychologist and an advocate of nonviolent resistance. He has founded several organizations including the National Youth Advocate Program in the United States, which provides alternative foster care and counseling to at-risk youth and their families; and Nonviolence International, which promotes peace education and nonviolent action in dealing with political issues across the globe. Before being deported by the Israeli Supreme Court in 1988 for organizing activities involving nonviolent civil disobedience, he was also a founding member of the Palestinian Center for the Study of Nonviolence in Jerusalem.

JAMES ARTHUR BALDWIN (1924–1987) was an American novelist, essayist, and social critic whose writings explore the unspoken intricacies of racial, sexual, and class boundaries in mid-twentieth-century America. His novels and plays bring to life fundamental personal dilemmas amid the complex social pressures bearing down on African Americans, and on gay and bisexual men. Such dynamics are prominent in Baldwin's second novel, *Giovanni's Room*, written in 1956, well in advance of the gay liberation movement. An unfinished manuscript, *Remember This House*, was expanded and adapted for cinema in 2016 as an Academy Award–nominated documentary film, *I Am Not Your Negro*.

WENDELL ERDMAN BERRY was born in 1934 in Henry County, Kentucky, where his parents' families had farmed for at least five generations. He is an American writer, environmental activist, cultural critic, and farmer, holding a deep reverence for the land and defending agrarian values. Authoring more than forty books of poetry, fiction, and essays, his poetry in particular celebrates the holiness of life and everyday miracles we often take for granted. He is an elected member of the Fellowship of Southern Writers, a recipient of the National Humanities Medal, and a 2013 Fellow of the American Academy of Arts and Sciences.

GRACE LEE BOGGS (1915–2015) "waged a war of inspiration for civil rights, feminism, the environment, and other causes for seven decades with an unflagging faith that revolutionary justice was just around the corner," according to her obituary in the *New York Times*. The daughter of Chinese immigrants, she was an author and philosopher who planted gardens on vacant lots in her adopted hometown of Detroit, marched against racism, campaigned for human rights, and founded community organizations and political movements inspired by her evolving vision of a revolution in America. Her journey took her from the streets of Chicago as a tenant organizer in the 1940s through academia and civil rights activism to her own manifesto for change, based not on political upheavals but on ethical values, visionary organizing, and grassroots community building.

BRENÉ BROWN is a research professor at the University of Houston where she holds the Huffington Endowed Chair. She has spent the past sixteen years studying courage, vulnerability, empathy, and shame, and is the author of four books. Her first TEDx talk, "The Power of Vulnerability," is one of the most viewed TED videos, with more than 33 million views.

TARANA BURKE, born in New York in 1973, is a senior director at Girls for Gender Equity and has worked with young women since her own teen years. She created the phrase "Me Too" in 2006 to raise awareness of the pervasiveness of sexual abuse in society and uses "the power of empathy to stomp out shame." The two-word phrase resurfaced on October 15, 2017, when actor Alyssa Milano took to Twitter to invite those who have experienced sexual harassment to respond with "Me too," which immediately got a huge response on social media. *Time* magazine named the silence breakers from the #MeToo movement as the *Time* Person of the Year for 2017.

OCTAVIA E. BUTLER (1947–2006) was an American science fiction writer whose novels explore issues of race, sex, power and what it means to be human. A multiple recipient of both the Hugo and Nebula awards, in 1995 she became the first science fiction writer to receive the MacArthur Fellowship for her novels, including *Kindred*, *Parable of the Seed*, and the Patternist series. Her books feature black women characters in hostile dystopias; Butler felt the genre of science fiction was a deeply appropriate vehicle for social commentary. Yet her books, concerned with empathy and the importance of building community, attracted an audience beyond their genre and were widely praised by critics. Translated into ten languages, her books have sold more than a million copies.

SISTER CHAN KHONG (TRUE EMPTINESS) was born in 1938 in the Mekong Delta of Vietnam. She began doing social work in the slums of Saigon as a teenager. In the 1960s she helped Thich Nhat Hanh set up the School of Youth for Social Service, which trained thousands of young social workers to bring aid to remote war-torn villages, and in 1969 helped him organize the Buddhist Peace Delegation at the Paris Peace Talks. In the 1970s she directed emergency efforts to rescue Vietnamese boat people from the high seas. For decades she has led sponsorship programs for orphans and poor rural schools in Vietnam and campaigns to bring relief to flood victims, the ill, and the hungry living in inaccessible and underserved areas of the country. In 1982 she helped establish Plum Village monastery and practice center in southwest France, and she is the most senior nun ordained by Thich Nhat Hanh. The deep mindfulness practices she has pioneered and developed (which she calls "social work of the heart") have brought reconciliation and healing to communities worldwide.

CÉSAR CHÁVEZ (1927–1993) was an American labor leader and civil rights activist who, with Dolores Huerta, cofounded the National Farm Workers Association (later the United Farm Workers union, UFW) in 1962. Originally a farm worker, his approach to unionism and use of proactive but nonviolent tactics made the farm workers' struggle a moral cause with nationwide support. By the late 1970s, his strategies had forced growers to recognize the UFW as the bargaining agent for 50,000 field workers in California and Florida. He has become a major historical icon, with many schools, streets, and parks in the United States named after him. His birthday, March 31, has become Cesar Chavez Day, a state holiday in California, Colorado, and Texas.

HIS HOLINESS, THE FOURTEENTH DALAI LAMA OF TIBET, TENZIN GYATSO, was born in 1935 to a farming family in a small hamlet located in Taktser, Amdo, northeastern Tibet. Living in exile in Dharamsala, India, since 1959, he is recognized internationally for his consistent advocacy of nonviolence, even in the face of extreme aggression. In 1989 he was awarded the Nobel Peace Prize for his nonviolent struggle for the liberation of Tibet. His Holiness has travelled to more than sixty-seven countries spanning six continents. He has received over 150 awards, honorary doctorates, and prizes in recognition of his message of peace, nonviolence, interreligious understanding, universal responsibility, and compassion. He has also authored or coauthored more than 110 books.

SISTER DANG NGHIEM was born in central Vietnam in 1968 during the Tet Offensive. Raised by her grandmother in Vietnam, she came to the United States in 1985, graduated in medicine from the University of California, San Francisco, and worked as a doctor. Ordained as a nun by Thich Nhat Hanh in 2000, she has integrated Western and Eastern medical traditions and shares the healing power of mindful awareness and nondiscrimination in her books *Healing: A Woman's Journey from Doctor to Nun* and *Mindfulness as Medicine: A Story of Healing Body and Spirit.* She is the abbess of Deer Park Monastery in Escondido.

ANGELA DAVIS, born in Birmingham, Alabama in 1944, is a social critic, political activist, academic, and author. She emerged as a Birmingham counterculture activist in the 1960s through her involvement in the Civil Rights Movement. She is professor emerita at the University of California, Santa Cruz, in its History of Consciousness Department and a former director of the university's Feminist Studies department. She cofounded Critical Resistance, an organization working to abolish the prison-industrial complex.

LOUISE ERDRICH was born in 1954 in Little Falls, Minnesota. A writer of novels, poetry, and children's books featuring Native American characters and settings, she received the National Book Award for Fiction for her novel *The Round House*. She is a member of the Turtle Mountain Band of Chippewa Indians, a band of the Anishinaabe, and she owns Birchbark Books, a small independent bookstore in Minneapolis that focuses on Native American literature and the Native community in the Twin Cities area.

LESLIE FEINBERG (1949–2014) was an American transgender activist, speaker, and author. She was a managing editor of *Workers World* newspaper; she wrote fiercely on behalf of those she saw as oppressed because of their sexual, ethnic, racial, or other identities. Her fiction, including her best-known and most influential work *Stone Butch Blues*, a coming-of-age novel, created space for others to express their own sexual and gender identities. Feinberg was awarded an honorary doctorate from Starr

King School for the Ministry for her transgender and social justice work.

MOHANDAS KARAMCHAND GANDHI (1869–1948) was the leader of the Indian independence movement against British rule. Born in Gujarat and trained as a barrister in London, he first employed nonviolent civil disobedience as a lawyer in the Indian community's struggle for civil rights in South Africa. After his return to India in 1915, he organized peasants, farmers, and urban laborers to protest against excessive land tax and discrimination. Assuming leadership of the Indian National Congress in 1921, Gandhi led nationwide campaigns for various social causes and for achieving Swaraj or self-rule. By employing nonviolent civil disobedience, Gandhi inspired movements for civil rights and freedom across the world. He was a revolutionary leader not only in politics, but also in spirituality, and it was for his devotion to the sacred principles of truth and love that he was given the title Mahatma or "great soul."

ALICIA GARZA, born in 1981, is an activist and writer in Oakland, California. She has organized around the issues of healthcare, rights for domestic workers, ending police brutality, anti-racism, and violence against trans and gender-nonconforming people of color. Together with Opal Tometi and Patrisse Cullors she cofounded the Black Lives Matter movement in 2013. Garza is credited with inspiring its name and slogan when, after the July 2013 acquittal of George Zimmerman for the murder of Trayvon Martin, she posted on Facebook: "Black people. I love you. I love us. Our lives matter, Black Lives Matter," which Cullors then shared with the hashtag #BlackLives-Matter. In 2017 Black Lives Matter was awarded the Sydney Peace Prize.

MONA HAYDAR grew up in Flint, Michigan, and lived in Damascus, Syria, where she studied Arabic and Islamic spirituality. She lives in New York City, where she is studying for her master's degree in theology. She is a rapper, poet, permaculture practitioner, meditator, and spiritual activist. Her direct actions include Ask A Muslim, in which she and her husband set up a stand in Cambridge, Massachusetts, with signs that read "Talk to a Muslim," "Free Conversation," and "Free Coffee and Donuts," encouraging open and loving dialogue with passersby, garnering the attention of NPR, *People* magazine, Al Jazeera, and other media outlets.

JULIA BUTTERFLY HILL was born in Mount Vernon, Missouri, in 1974. She spent more than two years living high up in the canopy of Luna, an ancient redwood tree in Humboldt County, California, to prevent loggers from cutting it down and to raise awareness of the plight of old-growth forests. Raised in a camper until she was ten years old by her father, a traveling Christian minister, as an adult she found spirituality in nature. She later founded the Circle of Life Foundation and travels extensively, speaking on environmental and social justice issues.

BELL HOOKS is the pen name of Gloria Jean Watkins, an American author, teacher, academic, feminist, and social activist. She was born in Hopkinsville, Kentucky, in 1952 to a working-class family and educated in segregated schools; as an adult, she has taught at Yale, Oberlin, the New School, and City College of New York. In a career spanning four decades, her work has centered on identifying and challenging systems of oppression and discrimination that are based on race, sex, and class. Using a writing style that defies academic conventions with its informality, her intention is to make her work inclusive and accessible to everyone, regardless of their class, education, or literacy.

DOLORES CLARA FERNÁNDEZ HUERTA, born in 1930 in the mining town of Dawson, New Mexico, is an American labor leader and civil rights activist who was the cofounder of the National Farmworkers Association, which later became the United Farm Workers. Huerta has received numerous awards for her community service and advocacy for workers, immigrants, and women, including the Presidential Medal of Freedom. In 1993, she became the first Latina woman to be inducted into the National Women's Hall of Fame. Huerta is the originator of the phrase, "*Sí se puede*," or "Yes, we can."

MUSHIM PATRICIA IKEDA, born in 1954, is a Buddhist teacher, author, mentor, and community activist based in Oakland, California. She teaches meditation retreats for people of color, women, and social justice activists and is a diversity and inclusion facilitator. Her work is based in values of cultural humility, acknowledging the wisdom that is ever-present in individuals and collectives, and the need for expression, empowerment, and cocreative self-determination in marginalized communities. She is also the recipient of the 2014 Gil A. Lopez Peacemaker Award from the Association for Dispute Resolution of Northern California, recognizing her innovative one-year program, Practice in Transformative Action (PiTA), a mindfulness training for social justice activists, at East Bay Meditation Center.

KABIR, born in Varanasi, India, was a fifteenth-century mystic and poet who has been beloved by Hindus, Muslims, and Sikhs. His teacher was the Hindu bhakti leader Ramananda. Kabir believed that God is within and he was critical of blind adherence to any religious practices he considered to be meaningless. His poems, composed in vernacular Hindi with elements of various dialects, were sung and transmitted orally until they were written down in the seventeenth century, and they continue to be sung today.

MARTIN LUTHER KING, JR. (1929–1968) is celebrated worldwide for his advancement of civil rights using the tactics of nonviolence and civil disobedience. Inspired by his Christian faith and the example of Mahatma Gandhi, he helped organize many campaigns, beginning with the 1955 Montgomery bus boycott. He cofounded the Southern Christian Leadership Conference (SCLC) in 1957, helped organize the 1963 nonviolent protests in Birmingham, Alabama, and the 1963 March on Washington, where he delivered his legendary "I Have a Dream" speech. On October 14, 1964, he received the Nobel Peace

Prize for combatting racial inequality through nonviolent resistance. In 1965, he coorganized the Selma to Montgomery marches for voting rights, and in the final years of his life, King expanded his focus to include opposition to the Vietnam War. In 1968, he was planning an occupation of Washington, DC, to be called the Poor People's Campaign, when he was assassinated on April 4 in Memphis, Tennessee. After his death, Dr. King was awarded the Presidential Medal of Freedom and the Congressional Gold Medal.

JACK KORNFIELD was born in 1945 and trained as a monk in Thailand, Burma, and India, primarily under the guidance guidance of the Venerable Ajahn Chah and the Venerable Mahasi Sayadaw. He has taught meditation worldwide since 1974 and is one of the key teachers to introduce Buddhist mindfulness practice to the United States. A psychotherapist by training, he has brought the insights of his profession to the practice of insight meditation and helped students in their understanding of the Dharma. Together with Sharon Salzberg and Joseph Goldstein, he is a founding teacher of the Insight Meditation Society in Massachusetts and Spirit Rock Meditation Center in California. His many books have sold more than a million copies and been translated into twenty languages.

SISTER ANNABEL LAITY, also known as Sister Chan Duc (True Virtue), was born in England and is a nun in the Vietnamese Zen tradition of Thich Nhat Hanh. She studied Classics and Sanskrit before going to India to live and practice meditation with a community of Tibetan nuns. She has been a disciple of Thich Nhat Hanh since 1986, and in 1988 became the first European woman to be ordained in his monastic tradition. She has translated many books by Thich Nhat Hanh from Vietnamese to English. Sister Annabel was ordained as a Dharma teacher in 1990, and was Director of Practice at Plum Village for many years. In 2000, she became the first European nun to give Buddhist teachings in Thailand. She is currently Dean of Practice at the European Institute of Applied Buddhism in Germany and she travels widely, teaching and leading meditation retreats.

WINONA LADUKE was born in Los Angeles in 1959. She is an environmentalist, economist, and writer, known for her work on tribal land claims and preservation, as well as sustainable development. In 1996 and 2000, she ran for vice president as the nominee of the Green Party of the United States, on a ticket headed by Ralph Nader. She is the executive director of Honor the Earth, a Native environmental advocacy organization that played an active role in the Dakota Access Pipeline protests.

AUDRE LORDE was born in New York City in 1934 to Caribbean immigrant parents, her father from Barbados and her mother from the island of Carriacou, and went on to become a leading poet and essayist who gave voice to issues of race, class, gender, and sexuality. She began writing poetry as a teenager, and her work created a language for others to honor and explore the "dark place within where hidden and growing our true spirit rises."

LI MAIZI was born in 1989. She is a Chinese campaigner and activist for gender equality and sexual identity. During her second year of university, Li Maizi set up a lesbian community-training group for students, offering counselling services and support. She was arrested by police on the eve of International Women's Day in 2015, along with four other activists, after a criminal investigation into their plans to hand out stickers and flyers denouncing sexual harassment on public transport. The Feminist Five, as they came to be known, were kept in detention for thirty-seven days, and were released after an outpouring of national and international support. Her current campaign work focuses on preventing forced marriage.

WANGARI MUTA MAATHAI (1940–2011) was a renowned Kenyan environmental political activist. In 2004, she became the first African woman to receive the Nobel Peace Prize; she had also been the first woman from East Africa to receive a doctorate (in biology), and the first female professor ever in her home country of Kenya. In 1977 she started the grassroots Green Belt Movement aimed at countering the deforestation that was threatening people's means of subsistence, encouraging women to plant trees in their local environment and to think ecologically. It spread to other African countries and contributed to the planting of over thirty million trees. Maathai's mobilization of African women was part of a broad vision that included democracy, women's rights, and international solidarity as well as sustainable development.

NELSON ROLIHLAHLA MANDELA (1918–2013) was a South African anti-apartheid revolutionary and political leader, who served as his country's first black head of state—and the first elected in a fully representative democratic election—from 1994 to 1999. Prior to his rise to power, he was in the twenty-eighth year of serving a life sentence in prison, accused of conspiring to overthrow the state. Although he was deemed controversial during much of his life, with critics on the right denouncing him as a terrorist and those on the left seeing him as too ready to negotiate and reconcile with enemies, he gained international acclaim for his commitment to peace and reconciliation. On jointly receiving the Nobel Peace Prize in 1993 with his former opponent F. W. de Klerk, he became an icon of social justice and democracy.

HEATHER LYN MANN, born in Chicago on the shore of Lake Michigan, is a spiritual ecologist and practitioner of mindfulness, sailing, and environmental advocacy. She founded and led the Center for Resilient Cities—an organization mobilizing city residents to restore natural beauty and function in damaged neighborhood landscapes. In 2007, together with her husband and cat, she set sail on a six-year, 15,000-nautical-mile ocean voyage, which became the subject of her 2016 book, *Ocean of Insight: A Sailor's Voyage from Despair to Hope*.

SUHAIYMAH MANZOOR-KHAN belongs to the third generation of a Pakistani family living in England. She was born in 1994 in Bradford and raised in Leeds, graduating with a history degree from Cambridge University and a master's in postcolonial studies from SOAS. In a witty, frank, and affectionate voice, she writes and speaks about politics, race, gender, feminism, Islam, being visibly Muslim, and Eurocentric academia, pointing at the absurdity of injustice in our everyday lives.

GABRIEL GARCÍA MÁRQUEZ (1927–2014) was a Colombian novelist, short-story writer, screenwriter, and journalist. He left law school for a career in journalism, and from his early days showed no inhibitions in his criticism of Colombian and foreign politics. He is best known for innovating the style of magical realism in his novels, and he was awarded the Nobel Prize for Literature in 1982.

XIUHTEZCATL MARTINEZ, born in 2000 in Colorado, is an indigenous climate activist, hip-hop artist, and powerful voice on the frontlines of a global youth-led environmental movement. He is the youth director of Earth Guardians, a worldwide conservation organization, and the author of the 2017 book *We Rise: The Earth Guardians Guide to Building a Movement That Restores the Planet*.

THOMAS MERTON (1915–1968) was an American Catholic writer, theologian, and mystic. A Trappist monk of the Abbey of Gethsemani in Kentucky, he was a keen proponent of interfaith understanding, pioneering dialogue with Buddhist spiritual teachers, including His Holiness the Dalai Lama, D. T. Suzuki, Ven. Buddhadasa, and Thich Nhat Hanh. He wrote more than seventy books on spirituality, social justice, and pacifism, as well as many essays and reviews. His 1948 autobiography *The Seven*

Storey Mountain inspired many veterans to seek spirituality at monasteries across the US after World War II.

HAYAO MIYAZAKI, born in 1941, is a Japanese film director, storyteller, manga artist, and animator. His works explore themes such as humanity's relationship with nature and technology, the wholesomeness of natural and traditional patterns of living, and the difficulty of maintaining a pacifist ethic in a violent world. His films include *Nausicaä of the Valley of the Wind*, *My Neighbor Totoro*, *Princess Mononoke*, and *Spirited Away*. Although his films are for children, he has a wide following among adults and is widely regarded as one of the world's greatest animation directors.

GEORGE MONBIOT, born in 1963, is a British writer known for his environmental and political activism. He writes a weekly column for *The Guardian*, and is the author of a number of books, including *Captive State: The Corporate Takeover of Britain* (2000) and *Feral: Searching for Enchantment on the Frontiers of Rewilding* (2013). He is the founder of The Land Is Ours, a peaceful campaign for the right of access to the countryside and its resources in the United Kingdom.

TAI MOSES is a journalist whose articles, essays, and reviews have been widely published in the independent press. She has edited a number of alternative newsweeklies, including the online progressive news magazine AlterNet. Tai grew up on the urban border between downtown Los

Angeles and the wilds of Elysian Park. She has continued to explore the half-wild realm in which human and animal lives overlap, including in her book, *Zooburbia: Meditations On The Wild Animals Among Us*. She lives in Santa Cruz, California, with her husband, Michael, their dog, Arrow, and a number of cats.

KASHA JACQUELINE NABAGESERA was born in Kampala in 1980. She is an Ugandan LGBTI activist, the editor of *Bombastic Magazine*, and the cofounder and executive director of the LGBTI rights organization Freedom and Roam Uganda (FARUG). She is considered to be the "founding mother" of the Ugandan LGBT civil rights movement for publicly campaigning to end homophobia in Uganda, a country where homosexuality is against the law, when she was just nineteen years old. Despite the murder of her colleague David Kato, she perseveres in nonviolent human rights activism and has since won numerous awards for her work.

THICH NHAT HANH, born in central Vietnam in 1926, is a poet, peace activist, and global spiritual leader known for his powerful teachings and best-selling writings on mindfulness. His key teaching is that, through mindfulness, we can learn to live happily in the present moment—the only way to truly develop peace, both in oneself and in the world. His life has been dedicated to the work of inner transformation for the benefit of individuals and society. A pioneer in bringing Buddhism to the West, he has founded six practice centers in Europe and North America, as well as two in Asia and one in Australia. Both monastic and lay students apply his teachings on mindfulness, peace making, and community-building in schools, workplaces, businesses, prisons, and in local mindfulness practice communities throughout the world. He is a gentle, humble monk—the man Martin Luther King Jr. called "an apostle of peace and nonviolence."

YOKO ONO was born in Tokyo in 1933. She is a Japanese multimedia artist, singer, songwriter, and peace activist. She has presented the biennial LennonOno Grant for Peace to people and organizations since 2002, in honor of her late husband John Lennon.

PEACE PILGRIM (1908–1981), born Mildred Lisette Norman in Egg Harbor City, New Jersey, was an American spiritual teacher, mystic, pacifist, advocate of vegetarianism, and peace activist. In 1952, she became the first woman to walk the entire length of the Appalachian Trail in one season. On January 1, 1953, she adopted the name "Peace Pilgrim" and started a twenty-eight-year personal pilgrimage for peace, walking continuously, crisscrossing the United States carrying only a comb and a toothbrush. She carried petitions against US wars abroad and spoke wherever she was invited. She stopped counting the distance she walked in 1964, after she had reached 25,000 miles. A 1964 KPFK radio interview became the booklet *Steps Toward Inner Peace*, of which her friends published and distributed more than a million-and-a-half copies to a hundred countries in thirty languages.

AUTUMN PELTIER, born in 2003, is an Anishinaabe girl from Wikwemikong First Nation, northern Ontario, Canada, and an environmental activist. She was only eight years old when she gave her first speech about the universal right to clean drinking water. Since then, Peltier has worked as an advocate for protecting natural water resources, from signing a treaty against the expansion of oil sands, to lobbying world leaders for water protection at the Children's Climate Conference in Sweden. In 2016 she expressed concern about Kinder Morgan's expansion of the Trans Mountain Pipeline to the prime minister of Canada, Justin Trudeau. She was a 2017 nominee for the International Children's Peace Prize for her work raising awareness of sacred water since 2014.

ALESSANDRA PIGNI is a humanitarian psychologist who served with Médecins Sans Frontières in Palestine and China. She has since dedicated her efforts to understanding the connection between meaningful work and burnout. She has been a visiting research fellow at the University of Oxford. Her first book, *The Idealist's Survival Kit: 75 Ways to Avoid Burnout*, was published in 2016.

PLUM VILLAGE is an international Buddhist meditation center in rural southwest France. Founded by Thich Nhat Hanh in 1982, it has grown to become Europe's largest monastery. In Plum Village, mindfulness is woven into all daily activities. It provides a beautiful, simple, and nourishing environment in which to cultivate the mind of awakening. The resident community hosts retreats for thousands of participants every year.

MARTÍN PRECHTEL, born in 1951, is a dedicated student of eloquence, history, language, and an ongoing fresh approach. He was raised on a Pueblo Indian reservation and later went to Guatemala and apprenticed to a shaman. He survived the civil war there and returned to his native New Mexico to be an artist, writer, and farmer, and to teach at his international school, Bolad's Kitchen, offering a hands-on immersion into language, music, ritual, farming, cooking, smithing, natural colors, architecture, animal raising, clothing, tools, story, grief, and humor "to help people to remember and retain the majesty of their diverse origins while cultivating the flowering of integral culture in the present to grow a time of hope beyond our own."

ADRIENNE RICH (1929–2012) was an American poet and essayist and one of the country's foremost intellectuals. With a career spanning seven decades, she is one of the most widely read and influential poets in the US. From a young age, she displayed exceptional verbal prowess and mastery of form. She continued to reinvent and enrich her style, moving to free verse and weaving in everyday language. Beginning with *Snapshots of a Daughter-in-Law: Poems 1954–1962*, her work became more personal as she reflected on female identity and motherhood. In her poetry and prose, she explored issues of feminism, sexuality, politics, civil rights, social justice, and the anti-war movement.

DORIA ROBINSON is a third-generation resident of Richmond, California, and the executive director of

Urban Tilth, a community-based organization dedicated to building a more sustainable, healthy, and just food system through urban agriculture. Urban Tilth operates thirteen community and school gardens as well as a CSA (community-supported agriculture) program; the vision is to produce at least 5 percent of Richmond's produce hyperlocally, believing that physical, social, and economic health is dependent upon ecological health; the restoration of one depends on the restoration of the other.

DANICA ROEM, born in 1984, is an American journalist, politician, and musician with her metal band Last Cab Ride. In 2017, she was elected to the Virginia House of Delegates. She is the first openly transgender person to be elected to any US state legislature.

JALAL AD-DIN RUMI (1207–1273), was a thirteenth-century Persian poet, jurist, Islamic scholar, theologian, and Sufi mystic. His influence transcends national borders and ethnic divisions: for the past seven centuries Iranians, Tajiks, Turks, Greeks, Pashtuns, and Muslims from Central and South Asia have greatly appreciated his art and spiritual legacy; in the contemporary era his poems have been widely translated into many of the world's languages and transposed into various formats. According to the BBC and *Time* magazine, Rumi may now be the "best-selling" and "most popular" poet in the United States.

ATEF ABU SAIF was born in 1973 in Jabalia refugee camp in the Gaza Strip, where he continues to live with his family. He is a political scientist, a novelist, and the editor of

The Book of Gaza, an anthology of stories by Palestinian writers. His account of the 2014 Gaza conflict was published in English under the title *The Drone Eats with Me: Diaries from a City Under Fire*, with a foreword by Noam Chomsky; he has also written the novel *A Suspended Life*, which was shortlisted for the 2015 Arabic Booker Prize, as well as four other novels and two collections of short stories.

RINKU SEN was born in 1966 in Calcutta and immigrated with her family to the United States when she was five years old. She has spent most of her life organizing and writing for racial justice and feminism. She is the former president and executive director of Race Forward: The Center for Racial Justice Innovation, and publisher of the award-winning news site Colorlines. She has authored the books *Stir It Up: Lessons in Community Organizing* and *The Accidental American: Immigration and Citizenship in the Age of Globalization*.

SULAK SIVARAKSA was born in 1933 in Bangkok. He has initiated a number of humanitarian, ecological, and spiritual movements and organizations in Thailand and worldwide, and is the author of several books, including *Seeds of Peace: A Buddhist Vision for Renewing Society*; *Loyalty Demands Dissent: Autobiography of a Socially Engaged Buddhist*; and *The Wisdom of Sustainability: Buddhist Economics for the 21st Century*. He was one of the founders of the International Network of Engaged Buddhists (INEB), which was established in 1989 with leading Buddhists including the Dalai Lama, Thich Nhat Hanh, and Maha Ghosananda as its patrons.

ZADIE SMITH was born in London in 1975 to an English father and a Jamaican mother. She is a best-selling novelist, essayist, and short-story writer known for her treatment of race, religion, and cultural identity and for her novels' eccentric characters, humor, and snappy dialogue. Her books have received numerous awards, including the 2016 Welt Literature Prize for her "alert eyes and ears and a keen awareness of cultural and social influences," addressing in her writings "the coexistence of people of different backgrounds and religious value systems and traditions."

BROTHER DAVID STEINDL-RAST was born in 1926 in Vienna, Austria. He spent his teen years under the Nazi occupation and was drafted into the army; he eventually escaped and hid until the end of World War II. In 1952 he followed his family to the United States and joined a Benedictine community in Elmira, New York. After twelve years of monastic training, Steindl-Rast was sent by his abbot to participate in Buddhist-Christian dialogue, for which he received Vatican approval. His Zen teachers were Hakuun Yasutani Roshi, Soen Nakagawa Roshi, Shunryu Suzuki Roshi, and Eido Shimano Roshi; he received the 1975 Martin Buber Award for his achievements in building bridges between religious traditions. Brother David serves the worldwide Network for Grateful Living, Gratefulness.org.

BRYAN STEVENSON is the executive director of the Equal Justice Initiative in Montgomery, Alabama, and a law professor at New York University. He has won relief for dozens of condemned prisoners, argued five times before the Supreme Court, and won acclaim for his work challenging bias against the poor and people of color. He has received numerous awards, including the MacArthur Foundation "Genius" Grant. His projects include The Memorial to Peace and Justice in Montgomery, Alabama, which will document each of the nearly 4,000 lynchings of black people that took place in the twelve states of the South from 1877 to 1950. A related museum, From Enslavement to Mass Incarceration, will offer interpretations to show the connection between the post-Civil War period of lynchings to the high rate of executions and incarceration of people of color in the United States.

THE TAIZÉ COMMUNITY is an ecumenical Christian monastic order near Mâcon in eastern France. It was founded in 1940 by Brother Roger Schütz and its church, L'Église de la Réconciliation, was built by young Germans from the organization Action Reconciliation Service for Peace, after World War II. The community is composed of more than one hundred brothers, from Catholic and Protestant traditions, who originate from about thirty countries. Taizé has become one of the world's most important sites of Christian pilgrimage, with a focus on youth; more than 100,000 young people from around the world make pilgrimages to Taizé each year, where they are encouraged to live in the spirit of kindness, simplicity, and reconciliation.

MOTHER TERESA (1910–1997), known in the Catholic Church as Saint Teresa of Calcutta, was one of the twentieth century's most recognized spiritual leaders, inspiring millions with her example of selfless work for the poor, the ill, and the outcast. She was born Anjezë Gonxhe Bojaxhiu in Skopje, then part of the Ottoman Empire, now capital of the Republic of Macedonia. She left home at eighteen to become a nun in Ireland, and in 1929 arrived in India, where she would spend the rest of her life. In 1950 Mother Teresa founded the Missionaries of Charity, a Roman Catholic organization that now has more than 4,500 sisters in 133 countries. They manage homes for people dying of HIV/AIDS, leprosy, and tuberculosis; soup kitchens; dispensaries and mobile clinics; family-counseling programs; orphanages and schools. Members take vows of chastity, poverty, and obedience, and also profess a fourth vow: to give "wholehearted free service to the poorest of the poor."

CARLA TRUJILLO is from Las Vegas, New Mexico. She is a Mexican American novelist, editor, and former director of the Graduate Diversity Program at the University of California, Berkeley. She has lectured on ethnic studies at Berkeley and Mills College in Oakland, California, and taught courses in women's studies at San Francisco State University. Her writing includes the academic works *Chicana Lesbians: The Girls Our Mothers Warned Us About* and *Living Chicana Theory*; as well as her novels *What Night Brings* and *Faith and Fat Chances*.

TSOKNYI RINPOCHE, born in 1966, is a Nepalese Tibetan Buddhist teacher and author. His fresh insights into the psyche have enabled him to teach and write in a way that touches our most profound awareness, using metaphors, stories, and images that point directly to our everyday experience. He is founder of the Pundarika Foundation, is the author of three books, *Open Heart, Open Mind*; *Carefree Dignity*; and *Fearless Simplicity*, and has a keen interest in the ongoing dialogue between neuroscience researchers and Buddhist practitioners.

SPRING WASHAM is a meditation and Dharma teacher based in Oakland, California. She is a member of the Spirit Rock Teachers Council and a founding member and core teacher at Oakland's East Bay Meditation Center, the most diverse Buddhist center in the United States. As the founder of Lotus Vine Journeys, she is also a healer, spiritual activist, and writer. In 2016 she published her first book, *A Fierce Heart: Finding Strength, Courage, and Wisdom in Any Moment*.

HANIF WILLIS-ABDURRAQIB, born in 1983, is a poet, essayist, and cultural critic. He is author of the 2016 poetry collection *The Crown Ain't Worth Much* and the forthcoming essay collection *They Can't Kill Us Until They Kill Us*. Born and raised in Columbus, Ohio, he writes on music, culture, and identity. According to his website bio, he thinks poems can change the world, (but really wants to talk to you about music, sports, and sneakers).

ELIE WIESEL (1928–2016) was a Romanian-born American Jewish writer, university professor, political activist, Nobel laureate, and Holocaust survivor. He authored fifty-seven books, including *Night*, a work based on his experiences as a prisoner in the Auschwitz and Buchenwald concentration camps. He was involved with Jewish causes and helped establish the United States Holocaust Memorial Museum in Washington, DC. He also campaigned for victims of oppression in South Africa, Nicaragua, Kosovo, and Sudan, acting as a defender of human rights throughout his life.

OPRAH WINFREY was born in rural Mississippi in 1954 to a single mother. She has played a key role in modern American life, shaping cultural trends and promoting causes through her talk shows and books. Her range of media enterprises has made her one of the richest self-made women, the first black woman billionaire in world history. As much as she is a thought leader herself, she is an enthusiastic student of experts in the fields of health, happiness, and spirituality.

MALALA YOUSAFZAI, born in 1997, is a Pakistani activist for education and human rights. She is recognized for her personal heroism in bringing awareness to the education of girls in her native Swat Valley, where the local Taliban had banned them from attending school. In early 2009, when she was eleven, she wrote a blog for BBC Urdu about her life under Taliban occupation, and the following summer, journalist Adam B. Ellick made a *New York Times* documentary about her. On October 9, 2012, a

Taliban gunman attempted to murder her by shooting her in the head. The murder attempt sparked an international outpouring of support. Since recovering, Yousafzai has coauthored an international bestseller, *I Am Malala*, and in 2014, she received the Nobel Peace Prize for her work in education rights, becoming, at seventeen years old, the youngest-ever Nobel Laureate.

Sources

Adichie, Chimamanda Ngozi. "Now Is the Time to Talk about What We Are Actually Talking About." *The New Yorker.* June 19, 2017. Accessed December 24, 2017. https://www.newyorker.com/ culture/cultural-comment/now-is-the-time-to-talk-about-what-we-are-actually-talking-about.

Ai Weiwei (@AiWW). "If there is one who's not free, then I am not free. If there is one who suffers, then I suffer." Twitter, August 23, 2009, 6:38 p.m.

——. "Tips on surviving the regime: Respect yourself and speak for others. Do one small thing every day to prove the existence of justice." Twitter, August 6, 2009, 12:39 p.m.

——. "Ai Weiwei 'Does Not Feel Ppowerful'." BBC News. October 13, 2011. Accessed December 24, 2017. http://www.bbc.com/news/av/ entertainment-arts-15288035/ai-weiwei-does-not-feel-powerful.

——.*Never Sorry.* Documentary film directed by Alison Klayman. Produced by Expression United Media in association with MUSE Film and Television, 2012.

Alexievich, Svetlana. "Svetlana Alexievich - Nobel Lecture." Nobelprize.org. Accessed December 24, 2017. https://www .nobelprize.org/nobel_prizes/literature/laureates/2015/ alexievich-lecture.htm.

Angelou, Maya. *A Brave and Startling Truth.* New York: Random House, 1995.

Awad, Mubarak. Interview. Catherine Ingram. *In the Footsteps of Gandhi: Conversations with Spiritual Social Activists.* Berkeley, CA: Parallax Press, 2003.

Baldwin, James. *The Fire Next Time.* New York: Dial Press, 1963.

Berry, Wendell. *The Selected Poems of Wendell Berry.* Berkeley, CA: Counterpoint Press, 1998.

Blake, William. *Songs of Innocence and Songs of Experience.* Mineola, New York: Dover Publications, Inc., 1992.

Boggs, Grace Lee, and Scott Kurashige. *The Next American Revolution: Sustainable Activism for the Twenty-First Century.* Berkeley, CA: University of California Press, 2012.

Boorstein, Sylvia, Norman Fischer, and Tsoknyi Rinpoche. *Solid Ground: Buddhist Advice for Difficult Times.* Berkeley, CA: Parallax Press, 2011.

Brown, Brené. "The power of vulnerability." TED: Ideas worth spreading. June 2010. Accessed December 24, 2017. https://www.ted.com/talks/brene_brown_on_vulnerability.

Burke, Tarana. Quoted in Koivula, Adah Koivula, "8 Inspiring Quotes from Tarana Burke's Visit to Hofstra." Her Campus. November 2, 2017. Accessed December 24, 2017. https://www.hercampus.com/school/hofstra/8-inspiring-quotes-tarana-burkes-visit-hofstra.

Chavez, Cesar. "Cesar Chavez" interview. Ingram, Catherine, ed. *In the Footsteps of Gandhi: Conversations with Spiritual Social Activists.* Berkeley, CA: Parallax Press, 2003.

Davis, Angela. Interview with Sarah Van Gelder. "The Radical Work of Healing: Fania and Angela Davis on a New Kind of Civil Rights Activism." *YES! Magazine.* September 13, 2016. Accessed December 24, 2017. http://www.yesmagazine.org/issues/life-after-oil/the-radical-work-of-healing-fania-and-angela-davis-on-a-new-kind-of-civil-rights-activism-20160218.

Erdrich, Louise. *The Bingo Palace.* New York: HarperPerennial, 1994.

Feinberg, Leslie. *Trans Liberation: Beyond Pink or Blue.* Boston: Beacon Press, 1998.

Gandhi, Mohandas K., and M. S. Deshpande, ed. *The Way to God.* Berkeley, CA: North Atlantic Books, 2009.

Garza, Alicia. "A Love Note to Our Folks." Jan 20, 2015 *n+1.*

Haydar, Mona. "The More Beautiful World." Mona Haydar. May 1, 2017. Accessed January 15, 2018. http://www.monahaydar.com/2017/05/01/the-more-beautiful-world/.

Ikeda, Mushim Patricia. "I Vow Not to Burn Out." Parallax Press. November 06, 2017. Accessed December 24, 2017. http://www.parallax.org/vow/.

Ingram, Catherine, ed. *In the Footsteps of Gandhi: Conversations with Spiritual Social Activists.* Berkeley, CA: Parallax Press, 2003.

Hill, Julia Butterfly, and Ajahn Pasanno. "In the Language of Love: A Conversation between Ajahn Pasanno and Julia Butterfly Hill." Barbara Gates and Wes Nisker, eds. *The Best of Inquiring*

    Mind: 25 Years of Dharma, Drama, and Uncommon Insight. Boston: Wisdom Publications, 2008.

Khong, Sister Chan. *Learning True Love: Practicing Buddhism in a Time of War*. Berkeley, CA: Parallax Press, 2007.

King, Martin Luther. *The Words of Martin Luther King, Jr.: Selected by Coretta King*. New York: Newmarket Press, 1983.

Kornfield, Jack. "Spiritual Practice and Social Action." Arnie Kotler, ed. *Engaged Buddhist Reader*. Berkeley, CA: Parallax Press, 1996.

LaDuke, Winona. *All Our Relations: Native Struggles for Land and Life*. Boston: South End Press, 1999.

Laity, Sister Annabel. "The Six Principles of Harmony." Arnie Kotler, ed. *Engaged Buddhist Reader*. Berkeley, CA: Parallax Press, 1996

Larkin, Geri. *The Still Point: Dhammapada: Living the Buddha's Essential Teachings—A Contemporary Rendering and Stories*. San Francisco: Harper San Francisco, 2014.

Li Maizi. Quoted in Fincher, Leta Hong, "China's Feminist Five." Dissent Magazine. September 1, 2016. Accessed December 24, 2017. https://www.dissentmagazine.org/article/china-feminist-five.

Lorde, Audre. "Poetry Is Not a Luxury." *Sister Outsider: Essays and Speeches*. Berkeley, CA: Crossing Press, 2007.

Macy, Joanna, and Norbert Gahbler. *Pass It On: Five Stories That Can Change the World*. Berkeley, CA: Parallax Press, 2010.

Maathai, Wangari. "Wangari Maathai—Nobel Lecture." Nobelprize .org. December 10, 2004. Accessed December 24, 2017. https://www.nobelprize.org/nobel_prizes/peace/laureates/2004/maathai-lecture-text.html.

Mandela, Nelson. *A Long Walk to Freedom: The Autobiography of Nelson Mandela*. New York: Little, Brown, 1994.

———. "Make Poverty History" speech. "Mandela's Poverty Speech." BBC News. February 03, 2005. Accessed January 15, 2018. http://news.bbc.co.uk/2/hi/uk_news/politics/4232603.stm.

Mann, Heather Lyn. *Ocean of Insight: A Sailor's Voyage from Despair to Hope*. Berkeley, CA: Parallax Press, 2016.

Manzoor-Khan, Suhaiymah. "This Is Not a Humanizing Poem." Roundhouse Poetry Slam, 2017. The Brown Hijabi. December 23, 2017. Accessed January 15, 2018. https://thebrownhijabi

.com/about/.

Martinez, Xiuhtezcatl. *We Rise: The Earth Guardians Guide to Building a Movement That Restores the Planet*. Emmaus, PA: Rodale, 2017.

Merton, Thomas. *Seeds*. Boston: Shambhala, 2001.

Miyazaki, Hayao. Quote from interview. "Interview: Hayao Miyazaki." *The Guardian*. Guardian News and Media. September 14, 2005. https://www.theguardian.com/film/2005/sep/14/japan.awardsandprizes

Monbiot, George. "Our Selective Blindness is Lethal to the Living World." The Guardian. December 20, 2017. Accessed December 24, 2017. https://www.theguardian.com/commentisfree/2017/dec/20/selective-blindness-lethal-natural-world-open-eyes-environment-ecosystem.

Nhat Hanh, Thich. *At Home in the World*. Berkeley, CA: Parallax Press, 2016.

———. *Being Peace*. Berkeley, CA: Parallax Press, 2008.

———. *How to Fight*. Berkeley, CA: Parallax Press, 2016.

Nghiem, Sister Dang. *Healing: A Woman's Journey from Doctor to Nun*. Berkeley, CA: Parallax Press, 2010.

Ono, Yoko. "Book recommendations by Yoko Ono." Imagine Peace. December 16, 2016. Accessed January 15, 2018. http://imagine-peace.com/archives/3365.

———. Peace Pilgrim. Friends of Peace Pilgrim, eds. *Peace Pilgrim: Her Life and Work in Her Own Words*. Santa Fe, NM: Ocean Tree Books, 1982.

Peltier, Autumn. "Autumn Peltier Talks Pipelines." YouTube. December 08, 2016. Accessed December 24, 2017. https://www.youtube.com/watch?v=wEDqbzLFOlc.

Pigni, Alessandra. *The Idealist's Survival Kit: 75 Simple Ways to Avoid Burnout*. Berkeley, CA: Parallax Press, 2016.

Plum Village. Song lyrics. *Basket of Plums Songbook: Music in the Tradition of Thich Nhat Hanh*. Berkeley, CA: Parallax Press, 2013.

Prechtel, Martín. *The Unlikely Peace at Cuchumaquic: The Parallel Lives of People as Plants*. Berkeley, CA: North Atlantic Books, 2012.

Rich, Adrienne. *Women and Honor: Some Notes on Lying*. Pittsburgh, PA: Motherroot Publications, 1977.

Robinson, Doria. Interview. Kyte, Lindsay, and Lion's Roar Staff.

"Changing the World One Life at a Time." Lion's Roar. November 16, 2017. Accessed January 18, 2018. https://www.lionsroar.com/changing-the-world-one-life-at-a-time/.

Roem, Danica. Interview with Ellie Shechet. "How to Win An Election, According to Danica Roem." *The Slot.* Jezebel.com. November 16, 2017. https://theslot.jezebel.com/how-to-win-an-election-according-to-danica-roem-1820521897.

Rumi, Jalal al-Din Rumi (Maulana) and Shahram Shiva, trans. *Hush, Don't Say Anything to God: Passionate Poems of Rumi.* Fremont, CA: Jain Publishing, 2000.

Saif, Abu Atef. *The Drone Eats with Me: A Gaza Diary.* Boston, MA: Beacon Press, 2016.

Sen, Rinku. "Using Knowledge, Advancing Activism." *Vimeo.* Barnard Center for Research on Women. November 17, 2011. Recorded on September 24, 2011 at Activism and the Academy.

Sivaraksa, Sulak. *Global Healing: Essays and Interviews on Structural Violence, Social Development and Spiritual Transformation.* Bangkok: Thai Inter-Religious Commission for Development , 1999.

Smith, Zadie. "On Optimism and Despair." *The New York Review of Books.* December 22, 2016. Accessed December 29, 2017. http://www.nybooks.com/articles/2016/12/22/on-optimism-and-despair/.

Steindl-Rast, David. *Gratefulness, the Heart of Prayer: An Approach to Life in Fullness.* Mahwah, NJ: Paulist Press, 1984.

Stevenson, Bryan. *Just Mercy: A Story of Justice and Redemption.* New York: Spiegel and Grau, 2015.

Teresa, Mother. *No Greater Love.* Novato, CA: New World Library, 2002.

Trujillo, Carla. Quoted in Espinoza, Alex, "Faith and Fat Chances: An Interview with Carla Trujillo." *Los Angeles Review of Books.* December 19, 2015. Accessed December 24, 2017. https://lareviewofbooks.org/article/faith-and-fat-chances-an-interview-with-carla-trujillo/.

Washam, Spring. *A Fierce Heart: Finding Strength, Courage, and Wisdom in Any Moment.* Berkeley, CA: Parallax Press, 2017.

Wiesel, Elie. Interview with Oprah Winfrey. *O: The Oprah Magazine*, November 2000.

Willis-Abdurraqib, Hanif. *They Can't Kill Us Until They Kill Us*. Columbus, OH: Two Dollar Radio, 2017.

Winfrey, Oprah. "Full Transcript: Oprah Winfrey's Speech at the Golden Globes." *The Atlantic*. January 8, 2018. https://www.theatlantic.com/entertainment/archive/2018/01/full-transcript-oprah-winfreys-speech-at-the-golden-globes/549905/.

Yousafzai, Malala. *I Am Malala: The Story of the Girl Who Stood Up for Education and Was Shot by the Taliban*. New York: Back Bay Books, 2015.

Maude White

Hisae Matsuda

About the Illustrator

Maude White is an award-winning cut-paper artist. She is the author of *Brave Birds: Inspiration on the Wing* (Abrams 2018). Her work has been featured by *Orion Magazine*, *The Artist Magazine*, and *Art House Press*, among others, and exhibited in national and international galleries. Her shadow puppet designs appear in *The Happy Film*. Through her work, she hopes to create scenes and stories that comfort and give solace. She lives in the Hudson Valley in New York.

About the Editor

Hisae Matsuda is an editor of books on personal and community healing. She is especially interested in listening to voices that are not usually heard. Born in Japan and raised in London, she lives in the San Francisco Bay Area.

About Parallax Press

Parallax Press is a nonprofit publisher founded by Zen Master Thich Nhat Hanh. We publish books and media on the art of mindful living and Engaged Buddhism. We are committed to offering teachings that help transform suffering and injustice. Our aspiration is to contribute to collective insight and awakening, bringing about a more joyful, healthy, and compassionate society.

Acknowledgments

My thanks go to this beautiful Earth and all beings; to my family and friends, without whom I would not exist; to my teachers, Thay Thich Nhat Hanh, and members of the Plum Village community; to Maude White, for helping me see beauty; to my colleagues at Parallax Press, Terry Barber, Jacob Surpin, Terri Saul, Heather Harrison, Stephen Houghton, Steven Low, Leslie Schneider, Earlita Chenault, and Nancy Fish, for your creativity and courage; and to Rachel Neumann for your audacious heart.

—Hisae Matsuda

This book would not have been possible without the patience, care, and energy of many loving and inspiring beings. I must thank my mother for her thoughtful perspective and her artistic eye, and my father for his unwavering support and his belief in my ability. Catherine, for her gentle spirit and voice. Joan, for her passion and resilience. Hisae, for selecting and honoring the words of these courageous leaders of love. Terri, Rachel, and everyone at Parallax for allowing me this opportunity to create alongside them—I am awed and inspired by the work you do and it has been such a privilege bringing these illustrations into being. Francie, for being patient with me, and for being my companion. Finally, and most importantly, I must thank all of the activists. I am inspired. I will do good. I will spread love.

—Maude White

31901063726667